THE PRETEXT

D1598835

BOOKS BY RAE ARMANTROUT

Extremities (The Figures, 1978)
The Invention of Hunger (Tuumba, 1979)
Precedence (Burning Deck, 1985)
Necromance (Sun & Moon Press, 1991)
Couverture (Les Cashiers de Royaumont, 1991)
[in French, trans. by Denis Dormoy]
Made to Seem (Sun & Moon Press, 1995)
writing the plot without sets (Chax Press, 1998)
True (Atelos, 1998)
The Pretext (Green Integer, 2001)

THE PRETEXT

Rae Armantrout

GREEN INTEGER
KØBENHAVN
& LOS ANGELES
2001

GREEN INTEGER BOOKS
Edited by Per Bregne
København/Los Angeles

Distributed in the United States by Consortium Book
Sales and Distribution, 1045 Westgate Drive, Suite 90
Saint Paul, Minnesota 55114-1065

(323) 857-1115/http://www.greeninteger.com

First Green Integer Edition 2001
©2001 by Rae Armantrout
Back cover copy ©2001 by Green Integer

Design: Per Bregne
Typography: Guy Bennett
Cover: Photograph of Rae Armantrout by Nancy Wolfing

Some of these poems previously appeared in the magazines *a.bacus*,
*Boxkite, Conjunctions, The Iowa Review, New American Writing,
Prosodia, The Provincetown Review, Raddle Moon*, and *Sulfur*
and in the books *American Poets Say Goodbye to the Twentieth Century*
(Four Walls Eight Windows), *Moving Borders: Three Decades
of Innovative Writing by Women* (Talisman) and
writing the plot about sets (Chax Press).

Publication of this book was made possible, in part, through matching
grants from the Literary Program of the Lannan Foundation
and the California Arts Council

LIBRARY OF CONGRESS CATALOGING IN PUBLICATION DATA
Armantrout, Rae [1947]
The Pretext
ISBN: 1-892295-39-3
p. cm — Green Integer 33
I. Title II. Series

CONTENTS

BIRTHMARK: The Pretext

You want something; that's the pretext. I recently abandoned a dream narrative called "Mark." You can see it, since you asked.

MARK

I'm with three friends.
We've parked in a lot downtown,
lucky to get a slot.

My son's friend
asks him if he's divided
his homework in three parts;
luckily he has.

Suddenly, I'm the teacher.
I see a line of Milton's.
I'm glad I haven't marked it wrong;
at first I thought it didn't fit.

That's not very interesting or it's only interesting because it's real. It's a real dream composed of three banal vignettes in which the same elements appear: luck, parts, and fit. It's interesting to the extent that the divisions and the fitting together arise spontaneously, without pretext. In other words, to the extent that there is a stranger in my head arranging things for me. Of course, I divided the *poem* in three parts. I chose the word *lucky*.

I have a real birthmark: a large red one on my outer left thigh. When I was a child, my mother referred to it as a "strawberry mark," with seeming affection. Was that some kind of trick? Because of what she called it, the mark has never troubled me.

I didn't mind having small breasts either, though in that case there *were* negative terms attached. Flat-chested, etc. But gender is the birthmark which has bothered me. When I was a child, Marilyn Monroe was the Sex Queen. I know people feel kindly toward "Marilyn," but I saw something horrific in

her act. Brilliantly horrific, maybe. She turned a
magnifying glass on the problem. Those unwieldy
bosoms held together by the weak "spaghetti
straps." Tee-hee. Something was inadequate. The
squeaky little girl voice would never be able to
articulate all that matter. No mind could get
around it. So she would be a stranger to herself
(and what could be more embarrassing or excit-
ing)? Was someone ever lucky! We watched her
pretend to pretend to be transfixed in the
highbeams of our little girl stare. Funny how you
can be excited without fitting in anywhere. But I've
gone off on a tangent when what I wanted to do
was swallow my own pretext.

WRITING

The clerk half skips away in his jaunty-officious
hurry. Oh, he's telling me a joke about our
common inability to occupy two planes. What he
can't know is that I hate body language. "My life
had stood, a little speech, a clipped coupon."
Hell is unredeemed experience?

If I were dying in a hospital bed, would I get pencil
and paper to jot down passing thoughts? Not likely.
I, myself, was always a forwarding address.

But here's the joke: syntactic space predates and
dominates these words.

We must take reasoning tests
before passing
through a cut-out
arabesque
in the Islamic

facade beyond which
small boats wait
to carry us
to the icebergs.
We hunker down
with short pencils
in front of the ticket booth.

POLICE BUSINESS

The suspect
spat blood and said,
"I love you," causing us
to lose our places.
We had warned him once
that being recognizable
was still
the best way to stay hidden.

Harmless as the hose is turquoise
where it snakes
around the primroses —
those pink
satellite dishes,
scanning the columns.

Was that an incarnation there
when *say* connected
with *so*? (Was it
an angel
or a Big, Big Star?)
We're just trying to make sure
that the heart's desire
stays put.

STREAM OF

1

We begin with some surrogate mothering
from the Mozart quartet,

disembodied peek-a-boo,
playfully exaggerated caresses,

Does it look like the succulents
have extended us their pads?

Numberless! So far so good
unless we're looking up someone's address.

2

Up our own dress
with a dramatic leer?

Another synonym for "not really"
in the lingua franca

which dissolves in a close-up,
closing again behind us.

3

Any exclamation
might be an old outpost.

Flagpole on a traffic island!
Where have we heard that before?

A big flag panting,
forth and forth,

over the double
stream of cars.

"I'm so lonely. BooHoo," she said, laughing and rubbing her eyes with her fist. She was being sociable. When I left she asked, "Where are you going? You said I could do a rendition and not be left alone."

"You'll never be alone," I joked, "if you have the flexibility to turn on yourself."

I was free—if that meant able to depict desires. To prove it I would separate from mine, make them flail like puppets. Honky-Tonk Women. The rote quality of the late work was part of its genius: a glimpse into the dollhouse of the soul, right? My schtick was omniscience, which always makes a room look small.

HER REFERENCES

You have exceeded
the maximum
number of spaces
for this personalization.

*

In the dream
Art Garfunkel
calls her by name,

trying to make her
put him in context.

*

When her mother worsens,
she imagines the funeral
of a living celebrity.

Who would attend?
Why or why not?

Is this dream logic?

*

Surplus meaning
could be collected
and made into pathos.

*

"Lettuce, fresh
from the Coachella Valley,"

not that she believes
any such place exists.

*

She has turned her back on
Self-Storage,

wants neither
a small corral
nor a few
plastic horses inside it,

won't say whether
it was she
who took snails
for a ride
in a wagon

and sang "Oh Susannah,"
then, "Oh Mama,
I'm Susannah;"
I'm the one
being referenced.

*

A few traits
may've been dreamed up
to suggest a likeness.

"Hey, hey,"
two laugh,
conspiratorially,
because they've met
by accident.

THE PAST

Sound
as a drum
or tight as a drum? Quick!

Is recognition
sentimental?

She never thought
when she was waiting tables
that there would be null sets.

People come first, but
categories outlast them.

She said, "If you're gonna hire
 the dummies, I quit!"

She thinks
this may be one
of those waitresses here.

Someone has probably mixed up
recognition with hatred.

Is she holding
a grudge,
a seance
or a piece of bread

which she won't eat because
someone
has taken a bite of it?

ARTICULATION

1

With whom
do you leave yourself
during reveries?

The one making coffee
or doing the driving —

that is the real
person in your life.
Now that one is gone

or has tagged along with you
like a small child
behind Mother.

"No!" you explain
in the crowded aisle.

"Without articulation
there's *no* sense of place."

2

When I dreamed about flying,
it was as a skill
I needed to regain.

I'd make practice runs
and float high
over the page. Pleasure

was a confirmation.
I remembered the way
and I was right!

Still,
one should be patient

with the present
as if with a child.

To follow its prattle —
glitter on water —

indulgently
is only polite.

THE INSIDE

She said,
"He gave me a message
for all the patients. 'Take two
aspirins or two
other medicines.' That may be
incomplete. He's still around here.
I think we should wait."

*

Trim squares
of dying grasses
arc away

as if to say,
"as if."

*

Symmetry mimics
a life-form's
self-justification.

*

Just between
appearance and what
something else was —

      or elsewise?

I mean I

SCAPE

Junkmail, each day:

"Make sure

it's not important!"

*

A breath as a place-
holder,

as the sea
throws a loose shawl
over its margin.

Who made this wish?

To postpone withdrawal
by spreading oneself thin,

to splutter and go out
continuously.

CARRIAGE

1

The pronoun
has switched seats again
to show she's impartial,

her view
not framed by self-interest —

but to whom does she show this
and why?

2

"Only those who know the difference

between things
and wishes

deserve to live
forever,"

says the driver.

3

What we need is a way
to make dalliance
and overview one thing:

sunlight on wavelets,

the blurred
Pointillistic paradise
lost on us

in the fellowship of
these cells.

EXCEPTIONS

Like saying, "Neener, neener,"
when you really mean,
"Neither,"
only more voluptuous,
a slow dissolve.

Symmetrical wrinkles —
no, ripples —
spread
from the impact
crater
of the mouth.

O won't the scrim
make tendency
seem more like remembrance?

That's no loose flesh;
it's a fringe
of rain, hanging —
'70s style —
except now style
is something more,

like gravity again.

SOMEONE ELSE

There's nothing
so glamorous
as someone else
meaning
what she says,

given the likelihood
she's wrong,
that her conviction's
only apparent,

because "we'll never
know for sure" and
she is living proof
of *that* —
she's earned her place

in the market,
besides,
she's the thing between
us and the maniac

who's strutting
and yelling simultaneously,
"What's the big deal here?
What's the big deal?"

EXCHANGE

1

The trainer says, "Yes,
I will tickle and bite you,
Kiki, if you will
put the keys
into the refrigerator."
Kiki complies, but
"Does she *really*
understand language?"

2

I grind my teeth and scratch my skin at night. Last
night I dreamed I was giving my mother, or the
mother of my son's friend, a long expository tour
through a series of adjoining rooms.

3

After every second chip,
the first bird counters
with the sound for hinge scraping.
Dove in the eugenie
bushes, mocker
in the oleander. Transubstantiation —
that's where gouge
turns into dazzle. In extremis
there is only one sensation.

OUR QUESTION

Does the child-narrator say,

"I found this pen.
I'm going to see if it will write,"

in order to
go find help?

*

He turns and stretches,

then, seeing us
approaching him,

goes through these motions
again, more markedly,

inscripting.

*

The child-narrator plays
this trick:

the new wave turns
uniforms
into constants

the next one makes
a costume from turning.

*

We test his intelligence

by asking
our question
in another way:

"Which one is different?"

"How are these the same?"

NEAR RHYME

Do I regret *each* thing
 I recall?
Or regret remembering
anything uncalled for

and wrapping it up
as if as
a gift?

I resent believing
there is someone else present
while I think there isn't.

*

That young girl listening
to "Angel Baby"

on a pink plastic radio
while staring out her window
at the planet Venus

was conscious
of doing what girls do —

thrilled to correspond.

That is what it means
to be young.

I could make you want it:
The protein carousel,
pronouns.

So what if
self is
else played backwards?

*

He rhymes
the disparate

nuclei, each one
bow-tie on

"nothing really."

IT

1. THE ARK

How we came to be

this many
is the subject

of our tale.
One story

has been told
in many ways.

In the beginning
there was just one

woman
or one language

or one jot
of matter,

infinitely dense.

It must be so,
but who can believe it?

2. THE HOOK

"But what about…?"
she asks

and stops,
shrunken

to the impulse
to formulate

some doubt.

Body a question mark,
         soul a wire hook.

NO

He said the flesh
had been made into words.

In line
as it is in sentences —

suspenseful!
"Tourists flee Tomorrowland!"

One time calls for another
in a wild, breathless way.

The copula may take the form of a cable
or snake.

All our nouns
will be back momentarily.

We're so sure
we can even glance away

(look)
as if between lifetimes.

Bell. Volition. Vocable.

As if it were needless
to say

COLLAPSE

Oh, what's the difference
between having seen
Ben Hur and
having been
a Roman
in a past life
filled with moving spectacle?

*

When I look out your window,
we're the same man

but for the purple
vw bug
just now passing —

compact as the present
in the mouth of an anchorperson.

*

When Stu blacks out the city,
the Rugrats save the day
by releasing light
from the refrigerator

The gang rehearses
pregnant Lucy's hospital visit.

Might such consortia
have evolved
intracellular functions?

Dreams come true
for a mousy teen
who bombs again
but believes he's examining
evidence of a new life form.

*

Old symbols collapse,
forming black holes.

A yard strung with plastic Jack-O-Lanterns,
some filled with poinsettias.

Pictures of dolls
and of Hillary Clinton
taped face out
over the windows

THE TURN

A plane drags its banner,
"Modern Oldies,"

to and fro
in the distance:

the relatively calm lake
in which we see ourselves

shrugged off
steadily, every which way,

without suffering,
seeming to thrive

on succession now
as decades do. They

don't exist
until they're caricatured.

With nonstop
exits and appearances

to reflect on,
any attribute

looks like a running gag
as well as a splashy

sales pitch. "United
Colors of Benetton" —

the increasingly rare
Cedar Wax-Wing?

BETWEEN

The sky's ribbed
vanishing act
and solidity's encryption.

Gasping had always
conjured voyeurs;

now even shrinking
and shriveling didn't!

No one home
in the "Virtual Village?"

Between the quote marks,
nothing but disparagement.

QUALIA

Pole's shadow qualifies
asphalt
in its measured manner.

Where impact
has become tenor, that's
the length of time.

The redness
of red,

the sad way light
whitesides the tops of stems.

Duration, for instance,
is eerie.

And there can be
clear arrhythmias —

a wind-chime singly,
then a fluttering

faster than the heart
is such a tease.

You think you know them,

need to stay
where they're going.

THINKING

So I try to think
more about what I think
and less about others, you know.

Try to rebuild and just
do what I did.

I've definitely made improvements.
I'm bobbing up and down.

I'm not looking at them;
they're not looking at me —

kind of like.

*

Light slides
like saliva
over bobbing
webs and wires.

*

One says the nerves
are too underpowered
to account

for the recognition of
objects.

One goes down the sidewalk
in a string tie and bolero,

swinging his arms high
like a drum major,

ghost-of-a-prayer

kind of thing.

MY ASSOCIATES

You identify
with the body's
routine

until you think
it's your body —

like thinking
you *are* the clock.

Identity is a form
of prayer.

"How do I look?"

meaning what
could I pass for

where every eye's
a guard.

May passes
as the whole
air's bedizened
flotilla.

To echo
is to hold
aloft?

Then take any word
and split it,

make it soil itself
to seem fertile.

So nasturtiums
are the dirt's
lips.

Fecund. Cunning. (Cunt)

DIRECTION

Age as a centripetal force.

She can't hold the fictive
panoply of characters
apart.

Is *that* scary?

Origin's a sore point.

(When the old woman sheds tears,
I say, "What's wrong?"

as if surprised

the way Peter denied
he knew Jesus in the bible.

But Jesus too
refused to recognize his mom.)

We want a more distant relation

like that of Christmas tree ornament
to fruit.

ABOUT

What's the worst that could happen?

"Schools of fish are trapped
In these pools,"
Say the anchors

Who hang
On nursing home walls.

Reference is inimical,
We find out now;

Its Moebius strip
Search called

Vital
To security.

Just keep moving
And it's about a snake.

About how long

Should we be able
To recoil? Recall?

Our brothers
Were already changed

Into enormous birds
                    like those.

We're the target audience.

Both male and female
Woodstorks wade.

PART OF IT

1

I'm apprehensive near the top of the impossibly tall ladder beside the waterfall.

And when I crawl out onto the rock above, it's clear I'm expected to sail from crag to crag.

"I couldn't have done this on my best day," I tell the receding British tour guide.

In fact, the whole thing is simultaneously lived and narrated to him as good-natured lament.

2

My mother takes an interest in the twitters coming from a birdcage invisible from her bed.

She insists that Aaron build a wooden perch to hang on her patio at home (like the wood bar on the wall in front of her from which a clipboard hangs).

The next day she informs me all the birds are dead. I tell her it isn't so, but she doesn't seem convinced.

Later, though, she whispers that the birds are "part of it," along with the nurses and the television.

SETS

Scheduled:
a two part
investigation

Recalling
the investigation

*

These bi
furcated
ovals
stand up
from the clear red stems —

not like hairs,
not like soldiers —

in this quietness.

*

Time's tic:
to pitch forward
then catch "itself"
again.

"We're" bombing Iraq again.

If I turn on the news,
someone will say, "We
mean business."

*

Eyes open wide
to form

an apology?
Disguised as what
might be surprise

over the raised
spoon.

GREETING

That wood pole's
rosy crossbar,

shouldering a complement
of knobs,

like clothespins
or Xmas lights,

to which crinkly
wires rise up
from adjacent yards.

*

I miss *circumstance*
already —

the way a single word
could mean

necessary, relative,
provisional

and a bird flicks past
leaving

the sense that one
has waved one's hand.

THE PLOT

The secret is
you can't get to sleep
with a quiet mind;
you need to follow a sentence,
inward or downward,
as it becomes circuitous,
path-like, with tenuously credible
foliage on either side of it —
but you're still not sleeping.
You're conscious of the metaphoric
contraption; it's too jerky,
too equivocal to suspend you

And Nature was the girl who could spin
babies out of dustballs
until that little man
who said he had a name showed up
and wanted them
or wanted to be one

of a cast of cartoon
characters assigned to manage
the Garden
so even Adam and Eve discovered
they somehow *knew* the punchline:
the snake would swallow
the red bomb

Why is sleep's border guarded?
On the monitors
professional false selves
make self-disparaging remarks.
There's a sexy bored housewife,
very Natalie Wood-like,
sighing, "Men should win" —
but the only thing that matters
is the pace of substitution.
You feel like trying to escape
from her straight-arrow husband
and her biker boyfriend

You can't believe
you're on Penelope's Secret.
A suitor waits
for ages
to be hypnotized
on stage.

CIRCUIT

"Than, Than" rang the birds —
horizonless echoes —

and for a human
there's comment's protraction.

"That's a beautiful truck;
that would cost a lot,
                            wouldn't it?"

The silver tanker
leaving the station.

ALL

When you sing, "Mama,
rock me all night long,"
you really mean
what the words say

though your insinuating tone,
your "Ha!"
seems to stand for a secret.

You've concocted implication
just to make a difference,
just to make time
and divide yourself in two.

     The new guy sings:

     "Customer sees me
     walkin' by, grinning."

A voice carries
in the record store.

"I'm all old
and everything."

HERE

1

I'm here to recreate
the "fleeting impression"
that others once saw themselves

as repositories of experience.
In a dream,
I'm three old actors

known for playing in Westerns.
We're on a trek through wild country
to show how the past might have been.

A voice-over says that our saddles
are especially worn and rough-hewn.

t's supposed to be beautiful
o repeat a motif
n another medium.

A regular
dither
in the strings

approaching Apollo
Cremation. Out front,
fountains

make a statement
about the ability
to keep up one's end.

There's a boy down the street,
firing caps
as my son did

while a church plays
its booming
recording of chimes.

THERE

Is it sentimental
when a grandmother

with cancer complains,
"I'm just not a loner,"

and that word jumps forward,

Brando on a motorcycle
a long time ago?

*

The wind passes
shadows
over rolling scrub as if

the word "There"
were being repeated.

*

"Be there"
meaning exist?

*

People buy photos
of the famous
murder scene because

murder is context.

OVER

Roused, you ask, "Wasn't that…?"

A breath, a stitch,
a harpoon.

You throw like a girl!

REQUIREMENTS

So this is what the left hand did —

extend a green
bilateral symmetry
into the sun,
palms up,
over and over.

Neutrality is whimsical —
but this could be hunger
somehow disguised
as a reiterated list
of chores
accomplished long ago.

Just reproducing it
requires
all the concentration
you are: this
taut prong
holding forth.

SIZE

In Heaven there is no want

and we are Wants.

*

Shame
takes sides

with the whole
against the parts.

*

Burning sensation
conceived as central —

lodgepole
or stalk —

while a blow
must be distributed,

as in seeing stars.

*

"I thirst,"
somebody else
might say.

Expression
is for dying gods.

LIGHT

Not with an order but a question,
apropos of nothing.

Something answers "Dark" and "Light."

These two
new beings are startled and draw back

from the beginning of time.
Are you happy?

*

No exit but attenuation?

Sky barely
orange at sunset.

Pulled out slow and thin,
her voice

means an objection
so pervasive
cannot know its enemy.

*

The purpose of abstraction
is to discover how
two things
can constitute a recurrence.

> To obtain reversibility.
> Gravity is to memory…

STATEMENT

In my country
facts are dead children.

When I say "dissociation,"
I may have said "real-time action."

This is my given name:

Thirty-One Year Old
Prima-Gravida,

The Pokey-Puppy.

Words
can be repeated.

The Distractible Sparrow,
The Smallest District.

The Strictest Definition.

Astronomers know
a signal's
not an answer.

NOW

Space temps as an echo.

The interval
created by the existence of two
nearly indistinguishable points.

The difference
between g and d
when g and d are gone.

*

A little girl
was paid to sing
"The Good Ship Momentum."

Paid in mother-love?

Space temps as an echo.

Just one
knock at a door
when usually it's three.

*

The supposed interval
himself, herself,
in ringlets, tap-dancing.

Space temps as an echo.

What does it say?

What does it mean to say
                        so?

GREEN INTEGER
Pataphysics and Pedantry

Edited by Per Bregne
Douglas Messerli, *Publisher*

Essays, Manifestos, Statements, Speeches, Maxims,
Epistles, Diaristic Notes, Narratives, Natural Histories,
Poems, Plays, Performances, Ramblings, Revelations
and all such ephemera as may appear necessary
to bring society into a slight tremolo of confusion
and fright at least.

*

Green Integer Books

Abingdon Square María Irene Fornes [2000]
The Masses Are Asses Pedro Pietri [2000]
Gold Fools Gilbert Sorrentino [2000]

Green Integer EL-E-PHANT Books

The PIP Anthology of World Poetry of the 20th Century 1 (2000)
readiness / enough / depends / on Larry Eigner (2000)

BOOKS FORTHCOMING FROM GREEN INTEGER

Islands and Other Essays Jean Grenier
Operatics Michel Leiris
The Doll and *The Doll at Play* Hans Bellmer
[with poetry by Paul Éluard]
Water from a Bucket Charles Henri Ford
American Notes Charles Dickens
To Do: A Book of Alphabets and Birthdays
Gertrude Stein
Letters from Hanusse Joshua Haigh
[edited by Douglas Messerli]
Prefaces and Essays on Poetry
William Wordsworth
Licorice Chronicles Ted Greenwald